The Call of The Nether

By

Avya Jain

The Call of the Nether   Avya Jain

Copyright © 2025 by Avya Jain

All rights reserved. No part of this publication may be reproduced, distributed, or transmitted in any form or by any means, including photocopying, recording, or other electronic or mechanical methods, without the prior written permission of the publisher, except in the case of brief quotations embodied in critical reviews and certain other noncommercial uses permitted by copyright law.

The Call of the Nether   Avya Jain

Table of Contents

Dedication 1

Acknowledgment 2

Foreword 4

Introduction 6

Chapter 1 Planning an Adventure 8

Chapter 2 Adventuready 10

Chapter 3 Adventuready! (For real!!...) 15

Chapter 4 Adventuready! (I promise...) 18

Chapter 5 In the Netherious Shadow 22

Chapter 6 The Next 'Day' Surprise 27

Chapter 7 Problem Parrot 29

Chapter 8 That was something… 33

Chapter 9 Aren 35

Chapter 10 The Big Exploration 43

Chapter 11 Finding Nether Wart 46

(and other stuff) 46

Chapter 12 The (Illusionatic) Obby Run 53

Chapter 13 Chests guest's chests quests (tongue twisters are just crazy) 55

Chapter 14 Back Outside 66

Chapter 15 Cleaning 67

(And another two tests. DUH!) 67

Chapter 16 What's Wrong with The Portal 72

The Call of the Nether   Avya Jain

Chapter- 17 Keys Hunt 75
Chapter 18 Back to Paradise 81
Chapter 19 Dinner Party 85

Dedication

To my **Great-Grandmother,** you are the brightest star I look up at every night.

I know your love always surrounds me like sunlight and helps me Rise and Shine!!

This debut is for you—whose spirit strengthens me, and whose love continues to shower down from above.

May these pages honor your memory and echo the light you left behind.

Acknowledgment

Writing my very first book has been a big adventure, and I couldn't have done it without some of the most amazing people in my life. I want to say a huge THANK YOU to all of you!

First, a big Thank You to my **principal Mrs. Stacey Ta** for always inspiring every one of us to dream big and try our best. Your words gave me the courage to write my own story, and I Love You a lot.

To my **library teacher Ms. Amy Dixon**, thank you for letting me spend time in the library and helping me find books that intrigue my curiosity and inspired me. You always smiled and asked about my writing interests, and that made me feel happy and loved.

Thank you to my **homeroom teacher Ms. Durkin** for teaching me how to write better sentences, fix my grammar, and add fun details. You believed in me and said, "You can do it!" That really helped.

To my reading teacher **Ms. Petrikonis**, who taught me the most efficient ways of reading and recommended fun books to read. Also, you taught me smart ways to improve grammar that helped me with my writing. You motivated me to go up the stairs and become someone totally different.

To my **Parents**, I love you so much! You listened to my ideas, helped me when I got stuck, and gave me snacks when I needed a break. You're the best team ever.

The Call of the Nether   Avya Jain

To my **friends**, thanks for reading my story and saying that I am a gaming expert!! You made me feel proud.

Special Thanks to my younger brother Advay—even though you're super naughty, noisy, and sometimes hide my notebook, you always cheer me up, make me laugh, and even help me think of cool parts for my story. You're my funny little hero!
Thank you all so much!

Foreword

Dear Reader,

It is with great pride and excitement that I introduce you to "The Call of the Nether," the first published work by one of our talented young students here at Brunswick Acres Elementary School. At just ten years old, Avya Jain has done something many adults only dream of: she has written and published her very first novel — and it's an adventure you won't want to miss! In her debut book, Avya invites us to step into a world filled with humor, adventure, and a cast of characters that will leave you chuckling long after the last chapter. From the first pages, I was drawn in by her funny, and wonderfully conversational storytelling voice. You'll feel like you're right there alongside the fun-loving, adventurous foursome as they dive headfirst into the dangers and delights of the Nether. Every twist and turn comes alive through her vivid descriptions. One moment you'll be on the edge of your seat as our heroes face a Ghast attack, and the next you'll be laughing out loud at their witty banter and creative problem-solving. Together, they navigate the perils of the Nether, proving that friendship and a sense of humor can overcome the most daunting obstacles. Avya brings to life the fiery terrain, peculiar creatures, and the unpredictable twists that await our adventurous foursome.

The Call of the Nether   Avya Jain

As educators, we often speak about nurturing the whole child and encouraging students to explore their passions. Avya's journey as a young author embodies everything we hope to inspire in our students: creativity, perseverance, and the courage to share one's unique voice with the world. It has been a pleasure watching Avya's passion and literary voice develop over the years! I am confident that this is just the beginning of Avya's journey, and I couldn't be more honored to introduce her first masterpiece to you.
I couldn't be prouder of Avya and her accomplishments! So, grab your pickaxe and prepare to be transported to a world where danger lurks around every corner, friendship conquers all obstacles, and adventure awaits those brave enough to seek it! I am confident that this story will not only entertain but also inspire other young dreamers to share their tales.

Happy reading!
Warmest regards,
Stacey Ta, Principal
Brunswick Acres School

Introduction

Sam, Gregory, Elizabeth, and Olivia had been friends for ages. Well, reader, you know what I mean by ages, for, in this context, 'years.'
As we say, four of them were brave adventurers (and still are; nothing stops them), but what made them brave adventurers was the fact that they had big interests. But first, let me let you talk to them:

Sam: "Hi, I'm Sam. I am part of a group of adventurers who love to go around the world. See Ya!"

Well, Sam, that was quick. Anyways **NEXT!**

Olivia: "Hello, I'm Olivia. I am also a part of the group of adventurers. It's so much fun, why don't you join?"

Uh, okay, I'll see . How about **NEXT!?**

The Call of the Nether   Avya Jain

Gregory: "Hi, I'm Gregory. I'm the third member of the adventure group. Also, you can call me Greg. Meet up!"
Um, okay, Hi Gregory -er, I mean, Greg. **NEXT!**
Elizabeth: "Hello, I'm Elizabeth! I'm the fourth member of the adventurers; you can call me Eliza. See ya as you join our experience in …."

THE NETHER!

Join the gang on a wonderful and mysterious trip. I'm just hoping things don't get any worse (they won't), or will they?

Chapter 1
Planning an Adventure

It was a beautiful day in the Overworld. The Overworld, a world where the ordinary turns into magic; a world where nothing is usual, and adventure seeks all. Sam, Greg, Olivia, and Eliza were on a lakeshore picnic, eating pasta and cookies, while their parents were farther down and taking a walk to admire the beautiful lakeshore.

The gleaming water and fresh green grass made it more and more beautiful. As the quadro sat, the more they talked. "We've had a lot of adventures in the Overworld," Greg said and was also bored.

If there was something in the Overworld -"

"I know!" Sam interrupted. "I heard that the Volcano Alps were here somewhere."

"BOR-ING!" The other three shouted. "Volcanoes are definitely not something that someone would ever wanna explore. There are better options now anyway," Olivia said.

"I agree," Greg said. The lava rings around the Volcano Alps are burning hot. It's also soooo boring. "Volcanoes are made of stone," Elizabeth explained. "What can we do there anyways?"

"Fine, fine," Sam muttered. "I was just suggesting".

"I think I know something! I'm pretty sure the place is in the Overworld. It also has so much to find and explore." Olivia exclaimed.

"TELL US! TELL US! TELL US!" The other three chanted excitedly.
Olivia tried to hide a smile. "Um I don't think I should –"
"Why not?" Sam urged.
"Yeah, why not?" . Eliza jumped in.
"Tell us! Please!" Greg forced.
"Um, okay…. How about …."
"The Nether?"
The group froze.
They stared at each other.
Then they stared at Olivia.
Then, back at each other with the most terrific grins ever. Suddenly….
"YES!"
"LET'S DO IT!"
"THIS IS GONNA BE AWESOME"
Alright, reader. Now is the time to truly start up what you signed for. And now I am going to say it….
Join the gang as they explore….

THE NETHER!

Nothing is ordinary here, nothing is just nice
You need to buckle up, to win and rise.
Join them as they get ready! (I really should not give you these little spoilers…)

Chapter 2
Adventuready

At sunset, the four families packed up to leave the beautiful lakeshore. Then they planned to meet up at Olivia's since her mom and dad had a huge house just right for four families.

After arriving at her house, the four took their shoes off, took fresh, chilled water bottles out of the refrigerator with them, and went right upstairs to Olivia's room. They didn't bother sticking around for fresh fruit and dessert.

After that, they sat quietly for two minutes.

Sam was bored, so he started the talk. "So, uh, what is our place of exploration again? I forgot."

"Wow, already?" Olivia asked, slightly surprised. Then, she raised one of her eyebrows.

"Sarcasm," Sam said, annoyed. "Sarcasm. I was just being sarcastic. Do you not know what sarcasm is or something?"

"Anyway, the name is the Nether," Olivia marked, changing the subject. "And that is final."

The Call of the Nether Avya Jain

"But what materials and gears do we have to take with us?" Greg asked.

The group thought for a minute. "Eh, probably just gear of every kind, just enough food and, books, our computers, beds, materials, and skills to build a good and proper place to stay for a while," Greg shrugged, answering his own question.

"But where do we get all those things? I don't have all of that." Olivia said.

"Huh," Elizabeth wondered aloud. "How about.... we work together to round up the materials and supplies?"

"But how?" Sam asked. "Oliva just said she doesn't have all of those things."

"No, no, what I mean is, what if we collect all the things together? Like if we have those things, even Olivia. We could bring the things that we have, and we all need them!"

"Ohhhhh! I get it now!" Sam said. "We can all work together to round up the supplies."

"That's what I was saying," Olivia remarked. Then she smiled.
"But right now, we have one concern," Elizabeth said.
"What is it?" Sam asked her.

The Call of the Nether   Avya Jain

"We do not know about this place!" Elizabeth exclaimed.
"That's right!" Olivia paused.

"Oh, wait! We can go to the library!" Sam exclaimed.
"Yeah! We don't even know if it is in the Overworld, or if it is safe to go, or if it has different kinds of rare and cool items to gather and look at." Greg said.
"Wow, Greg," Olivia said, surprised. "You're so demanding." Olivia said this to tease Greg, but Greg took it seriously.
"What are you talking about? We're going to the Nether for an adventure and to find cool rare stuff!" Greg replied.
"I was just teasing you. Can't you take a joke?" Olivia asked Greg, trying to hide a smile.

Greg's face turned red, and he looked in the other direction, away from Olivia.

"Anyways, there's one more thing… Do you have gear? Because my family does not. But we do have some other things and crafting tables." Sam said and quickly changed the subject.
"We have everything else but gear…" Olivia started.
"We do not either," Greg said.

"We just have lots of diamonds, golds, bricks and iron bricks, and crafting tables and wooden blocks, and ch -"

The Call of the Nether   Avya Jain

"Okay, that's enough!" Eliza stopped him. "All we know now is that you do not have gear. We don't either..."
The group froze.
That's when Olivia came to her senses. She gasped, "Oh no!". None of us have gear, but combined, we have everything else! What do we do now? "
The group was silent. One minute passed. Then another. Then another.

Suddenly...

"Come on!" Sam said, disappointed.
"We can't do this now!" Olivia said.
"I'm so upset!" Greg said.
Then, the three of them turned to Eliza.
They watched as she tapped her chin in thought then she got up and started to pace around the room, still thinking.
Then she suddenly said, "Hey! I just realized! I read in a book that we can craft diamond gear with diamonds and a crafting table".

"Gold gear with gold bricks and a crafting table?" Sam asked.
"Iron gear with iron bricks and a crafting table?" Greg and Olivia asked at the same time.

"Yup!" Elizabeth answered.

Then their parents called. It was time to go home.
And now that they were super happy, they planned to meet at the library the next day at noon.
They could read and find out about the Nether and its requirements and if they could build a good-looking safe fort there.

They left Olivia's house very happy indeed.

Chapter 3
Adventuready! (For real!!...)

The next day started with each kid having glazed honey waffles at their own houses, which was totally coincidental. But there was something strange in the air that day. Time's speed was unmatched and everything seemed unlike. Nobody noticed this until now.

The quadro didn't realize that time was passing extremely quickly that day. In fact, they didn't even know when 12:00 pm appeared out of thin air. Nobody noticed it until they reached the library. But still, it was like 12:00 appeared out of thin air.

Okay, not exactly out of thin air. But still, you know what I mean. Anyways, back to the story...

When they sat in their cars for the library, Olivia finally started to notice it.

She lived ten miles from the library. It usually took twenty-five minutes, but she noticed it took one minute. When they reached the huge, all book-filled-with-nothing-else library, they all agreed something was wrong.

Then, suddenly, the strangest thing happened, something completely not ordinary. The four suddenly appeared on a soft cotton couch with books about the Nether in their hands. Kinda mysterious, isn't it?

"Huh? How did that happen?" Olivia asked herself.

"Exactly." Greg said. "Something's happening. Oh well, let's read these books."

Greg picked up the book out of the many in his lap called *The Nether and what to be aware of.* He decided to read that and gather the information that the group would need to know what was coming.

Sam decided to read the book called *All about The Nether and Cool Stuff to be on the Lookout for.*

He read that so he could know for the group what cool things were there for them to search for and possibly bring back.

The Call of the Nether — Avya Jain

Olivia read the book in her huge stack of books called *The Nether, How to Get There, and more.* She thought she would read that for the way to come and go, what kinds of maps to design and buy, and other stuff that would come handy.

Eliza decided to read the book called *Nether Signs and sounds* to know what creature was making what sound in the Nether, and if suppose the Nether would stop all its lava from flowing, they all would know what that meant.
So, they read and read. And gathered the worthy knowledge they needed. After some fast food, they left for their houses with the best knowledge of humankind about the Nether that they could possibly gather, and you know what they say, don't you: knowledge is the greatest weapon that is in existence right now. So ANYWAYS, after hearing me talk my absolutely BORING talks again, let's continue…

Chapter 4
Adventuready! (I promise...)

The four met in the evening at Olivia's house. This time, they grabbed a plate of fresh-out-of-the-oven brownies and dashed right upstairs to discuss their next plan.

"Okay, so we did learn a few things. I found out it's in the Overworld." Sam marked.
"So. that's good for us," Greg said. "I read, it has flat and safe land in some areas and lots of materials so that we can build a fort. But it does not have trees because of the random fires."
"Olivia, why do you seem scared to me?" Eliza said and glared at Olivia.

"Uhhh, I read it has weird monsters, so we're gonna need a lot of combat gear," Olivia said and quickly changed the subject.
"And I read it has a lot of cool, rare, and mysterious items to craft and collect, and we can also collect and craft the coolest and strongest of weapons in existence!" Eliza exclaimed excitedly.

"Also, don't forget! It's hard to get food and water there. So, we will have to stock up on a lot of different food." Olivia reminded everyone.

"Oh yes. Food. Can't see how someone won't forget that." Eliza said.

"I learned one more fact, and I think it's the most important one. We don't walk there." Olivia said.

"So?" Greg asked.

"We have to teleport," Olivia replied.

"But how are we gonna do that?" Greg asked.

"I think I know!" Eliza jumped in. "We use obsidian to make a 5x4 frame- "

"Wait a second!" Sam interrupted. "What's obsidian?"

"Obsidian is a shiny, smooth, black rock that is rare and hard to find," Eliza said, annoyed with Sam's interruption.

"So, as I was saying," Eliza continued, "We use obsidian to make a 5x4 frame. Then, we put glass in the frame and burn it using flint and steel, and then we've got a portal!"

"Wait again! What's a portal?"

"Ugh, it has to be Sam," Eliza exclaimed. "Well, a portal is something to use to get somewhere when the place isn't of walking distance."

"Oh, okay, I guess," Sam said.

"Dude, why didn't you just read the books?" Greg asked Sam.

"I did! The book had no information about portals or obsidian," Sam replied. Eliza rolled her eyes.

The Call of the Nether   Avya Jain

"So then what was the book about?" Greg asked. "It was only about the Nether and what we need to be aware of," Sam replied. "Anyways, what Eliza explained was exactly what I found in the book that I read," Olivia said.

The next day, everything was finally final... All the gear, materials, combat tools, and food had been stocked up and safely packed.

The group was indeed happy. Even their parents knew about it. Everyone was very happy.

The Call of the Nether — Avya Jain

Ecstatic, the quadro had finally built their portal- framed with obsidian with purple stuff swirling around in it.
"Whew!" Greg Panted. "That was a lot of work and trying!"
"Hey, it was mostly ME! Even though I didn't even know what a portal was," Sam said.
"What do you mean, you don't know that a portal is? Didn't I tell you some time ago?" Eliza raised an eyebrow at Sam.
"And now the teleporting...." Olivia paused. She looked at all the parents, including her own.
"Let's go." Sam urged.

And so, they did.

Chapter 5
In the Netherious Shadow

The four had not walked to the Nether- they teleported. But still, they were very tired and weary. They looked around.
Blazing fires flickered, creating a damp light which arose from the floor, which was all Netherrack. The GROUND was Netherrack, readers! Okay, WHATEVER…

"Okay, I never imagined it being like this," Eliza said, quivering.
"Me neither," Sam said.

The Call of the Nether — Avya Jain

"I think we should build a fort that expresses our talent when it comes to building with legendary materials right now," Greg suggested proudly.

"Good idea," Olivia replied with a smile.

They were prepared and excited to work, as they had experience with building for a long time and they thought it was really fun, because everyone wants to express their inner creativity while being unlimited. They began by placing one block at a time, chatting and having fun.

Olivia's eyes sparkled as she began to build with the pile of diamonds. She loved diamonds a lot and called to build with them right away. It started to gleam as soon as she was finished with her part of the fort-building. It looked like an ocean wave held in place.

Greg, as an iron lover, called the iron right away and built with it right beside Olivia's diamonds so that it looked just like an ocean next to some perfect stones.

Eliza, with her handy-dandy gold, built on the other side of the diamonds to make it look like ice with the sun falling on it.

Sam worked on the roof with strong stones and the fort started to look like a beach hut, except it was in the Nether. It looked surreal.

The Call of the Nether   Avya Jain

Then, Eliza decided they needed some crystal-clear and safe windows, so she added them to the walls to make the fort look crystal touched.

And then, reader, after hours of hard work, they had finally had their fort, completed with four beds and a big storage room for their food and combat.

"Whew!" Greg exclaimed. "That was certainly a lot of work."

Suddenly, a Ghost appeared out of nowhere! (ghost is a not too big not too small jellyfish-like creature that floats, except its head is a cube shape and the 'tentacles' are rectangular prism type shapes)

Sam yelped, and everyone switched from empty hands to diamond and gold swords and other types of combat.

"Go away, you pesky something!" Sam shouted and shot an arrow at the ghast.

"It's not a pesky thing, it's a pesky ghast!" Olivia shouted to Sam.

"Whatever!" Sam shouted back.

The Call of the Nether   Avya Jain

The group surrounded the ghast. The ghast was now confused. Th group saw their chance and started to shoot arrows at the ghast from every direction. The ghast flew away, thinking that if it didn't, it would be stuck there. With teamwork, the group managed to scare away the ghast.

"Um guys, don't you think that was a little weird? Olivia asked.
"Yeah, I thought so too," Sam said.
"Let's go to our new awesome fort and get some rest," Olivia said.
"Hold on," Eliza said. "I'm coming in a second."
Eliza came inside two minutes later. She had posted a sign outside saying, "The special quadro fort" in the most beautiful cursive.

The Call of the Nether   Avya Jain

"Wait, I have an idea!" Sam exclaimed.

"What are you gonna do now?" Greg asked Sam. "Tell us that we're surrounded by more Ghasts?"
"Are you crazy?" Sam said, as he looked out the window. "I don't see any more creatures. What I WAS going to do was get my camera and take a good picture of our fort from the inside and outside. Then, when we come back home from here, we have a fort picture to show to our parents!"

"Great idea, I guess," Greg muttered.

So, Sam went outside to take the picture when Greg decided to photobomb his photograph.
But luckily for Greg, Sam didn't notice it right away. When Sam came back inside, the quadro decided to get some rest and sleep.
HEY, it was literally best for them to get all the SLEEP they could possibly get, because they were going on an ADVENTURE and weren't possibly get a god sleep for a couple of days! Okay, WHATEVER. Back to the story, I guess.

Chapter 6
The Next 'Day' Surprise

The four woke up in the morning the next day. They stepped outside of their fort and saw the most horrible and weird sight. Everything was the same as night! Blazing fires flickering, making light in the elite darkness, Netherrack floors. Nothing had changed since they arrived at the Nether, which was a day ago!

"What?" said Sam.

"Huh?" But why can I hear some birds chirping?!" Eliza screamed.

"Can someone tell me that I am seeing things?" Olivia rubbed her eyes in great disbelief.

"Okay, I've lost track of day and night," said Greg firmly.

The group was pin-drop silent.

"I AM GOING TO REPEAT BUT CAN SOMEONE TELL ME WHY I CAN HEAR BIRDS CHIRPING?!?" Eliza **screamed again.**

Startled, Sam stepped back as Eliza's voice echoed through the maze-like walls of the Nether. "Because your ears are probably ringing?" he said and shrugged. "Maybe we should go back home. This place is NOT safe!"

"Are you being serious right now?" Eliza was devastated. "Even I wouldn't cut our adventure short just for this kind of little thing!"

"That's it. We are teleporting back home. Our adventure here is over," Olivia said and headed to the portal.

"Wait, already?" Sam asked, surprised that Olivia was acting so strange.

"Didn't YOU talk about something like this, Sam?" Eliza asked. Olivia stopped. Then she looked back at the rest of her three friends.

"Aren't you all gonna come too?" she asked them.

"Nope," the other three said in unison.

"This looks like an interesting place," said Eliza.

"I'm pretty sure we can find some cool and rare stuff over here," Sam shrugged.

"And, well, I'm pretty sure this place is worth an exploration and also an adventure," Eiza finished.

"Well, I'm going back home," she said to them. But then a strange thing happened. She took another step towards the portal, and it vanished in a swirl of purple.

The four of them just froze and stood there with their mouths dangling open like a door on broken hinges. They were all shocked, confused, and baffled. They were mostly devastated.

Chapter 7
Problem Parrot

"Wha- how did this happen?" Greg asked, of course, shocked. "Huh? But I didn't read about a scenario about something like this happening! I don't know what to do!" Eliza shouted at them. Suddenly, out of thin air, a bird with elegant white feathers came into the group's sight.

"Ooh, look at that." Greg pointed at the bird.

Before they could say anything, the bird began to talk to them. "All of you humans might be wondering who I am, so let me start with that and get to the secondary elements later. I am the Problem Parrot, and I live here in the Nether."

"Problem Parrot?" Olivia asked.

"A parrot with WHITE feathers?" Eliza asked.

The Call of the Nether — Avya Jain

"Yes, the reason I have white feathers is because I am a unique parrot, different from all others that you've seen," said the Problem Parrot. I come right after someone or something in the Nether has a problem".

So, uh, do you have the ability to solve the problem or something like that? You do, right?" Greg asked the Problem Parrot.

"No!" the Parrot suddenly shouted. "But it makes you look like you took over my job!"

YOU DARE DO SOMETHING LIKE THAT!?"

"N-no!" Greg stammered. I- I was just asking. I didn't know."

"What do you mean you don't know?" I told you a minute ago!" The Parrot looked at Greg like he had the IQ of a dirty gym sock. Will you ever be quiet, Greg?" Sam whisper-screamed at him and nudged him.

"Okay, okay, fine," Greg sighed. "I didn't know BEFORE you told me."

"Okay, THAT makes more sense, unlike what you said earlier about NOT KNOWING that I'm NOT HERE to SOLVE your problems," the Problem Parrot said.

"So, anyways, back to me, and **NO**, I am **NOT** meant to solve problems. I am only here to tell whoever has a problem that they have a problem". The Problem Parrot continued.

"So, **BYE!**" said Problem Parrot.

And with that, the Problem Parrot flew away.
The group was pin-drop silent. Again, after two minutes of silence, they decided to go to the safety of their fort, the same fort that they called 'super awesome'. Then they decided to rest for a while because the Problem Parrot took away most of their day. Well, NETHER day. But STILL! Okay, WHATEVER…
"This is the problem. If we keep making these little mistakes, that annoying Problem Parrot will be taking all our exploring time away," said Eliza. "We have to be really careful."
"What's wrong with that parrot?" Sam asked.
"I dunno," Greg replied. "But it's pretty clear that that Problem Parrot wants to, like, disturb us or something."
"Wait, how can you see THAT as a possibility?" Eliza asked.
"I'm just saying. It's at the top of my mind, so I just said it," Greg replied again.

The group was silent again. For about two minutes.
"I have no idea what to do now," Eliza said.
"Me neither," Olivia said.
"I know," Sam said. "How about we go exploring and try our best not to get any problems on our hands?"
"Are you sure you want to risk it? I am literally starting to feel like Problem Parrot is stalking us or something. Maybe it wants to get to us or something."

"Greg's got a point, "Olivia said.
Suddenly, a small white bird-like animal flapped into their fort. It suddenly started going bananas and pecking Greg's head with its legs and beak. Greg screamed so loudly that he might have shattered the diamond wall and the fort windows So did everyone else.

"AAAAAAHHHHHHH!!!! KILL IT! KILL IT! KILL IT!"

Sam screamed and rushed out of the main room, rushing back in with his diamond sword.
The bird saw it and stopped. Its eyes widened. The quadro gasped.

It was the **Problem Parrot.**

Chapter 8
That was something…

As I said, readers, the group recognized the bird and saw that it was the Problem Parrot. Readers, you might be asking, "What's the problem this time?" Well, the truth is, I can't tell you just now. You must find out. So, I will continue….

"Uhhhh….." Greg said. "Um, what's the problem **THIS** time?".

"**GLAD YOU ASKED**!!" The Problem Parrot screamed at him. "Let me ask you a very important question," the Problem Parrot said, looking at Greg. Greg was stunned.

"Who exactly were you talking about?" The Problem Parrot asked.

"Ummmmmmmm…... you?" Greg said with a shrug.

Sam angrily nudged him and then shushed him. Greg mouthed a 'sorry'.

"Uh, Problem Parrot? He was talking about YOU because, number ONE, we don't know why you are coming to us every time we have a problem AND, number TWO, why you just tell us that we have a problem and then just LEAVE?" Eliza asked the Problem Parrot.

"Well, I am the Problem Parrot. It's in my NAME! DUH!" The Problem Parrot replied.

"Okay, DUH! Not like I wanted to know that" Eliza said. "But I have something to show you."

She then got up and turned on her heel and exited the main room. The others, even the Problem Parrot, were sitting in silence. They were all stunned by Eliza's bravery.

Eliza went to her storage cabinet. She took out the book about the Nether that she had read at the library before they teleported to the Nether. Eliza reentered the room, with a really mad expression on her face, where the rest of her friends and the Problem Parrot were.

She sat on the couch and opened the book and said to the parrot, "If me and the rest of these three combine all the books in the Nether section of the library back at our home and read them all, we know that there is nothing about a Problem Parrot that lives in the Nether. I know that you aren't a parrot in particular. She said to the Parrot, "Reveal yourself before it's too late, or don't you even come and pester us again if we have a problem with it; we make a mistake. We will find out on our own. Got it?" You're probably a human, and I know that I'm not wrong. Just tell us who you really are, okay?" Eliza was only a nine-year-old girl, and she was going for the gold, Reader!

Chapter 9
Aren

"Alright, I guess," The Problem Parrot said. I'm an ordinary girl. My name is Aren".

"Well? Why didn't you just say so? We could have all been friends, you know?" Olivia said.

"Besides, why are you a parrot? And why do you live in the Nether? Sam asked.

"I'm a parrot because the Nether saw that I was good at investigating, so it gave me the ability. I can turn back into a human, too." Aren said.

She transformed and turned into her normal form: A girl.

Aren had honey blonde hair arranged into a ponytail, and she also had purple-rimmed glasses.

The Call of the Nether   Avya Jain

The Call of the Nether
Avya Jain

"I was living in the Nether because I was part of a five-person group of adventurers, and we came here seeking an adventure. When we came, a ghast came and suddenly attacked us.

It started shooting fireballs everywhere that I could look. It was literally blinding, because the light from one of those fireballs is ten times as powerful as the sun. It made my friends run everywhere, and they ran until they were out of my sight. I didn't see the ghast until after they were gone, and I didn't know where they went. But when I saw it, I knew it was too late, and I hid behind a wall until it was out of my sight.

I quickly went to the portal back to the Overworld, but it disappeared in a swirl of purple as soon as I was just a few steps away from it.

I ran as fast as I could to the center of the Nether for help, and it gave me the ability to transform into a fast-flying parrot.

Since then, I have been informing others of the problems that they have that are going to affect them because I didn't want them to be in big trouble like I am." Aren said.

The Call of the Nether   Avya Jain

"Sorry for being rude. I thought you were something, I mean someone totally different, but I guess I was wrong," Eliza said.
" No need to apologize. It happens," Aren replied.
"Our portal disappeared, too," Sam said.
"Really?" Aren said, surprised.
"Ours-I mean, mine -disappeared too! I suppose there is something going on with the portals in the Nether." Aren continued.
"Well, you can always be part of us. We'll make you an extra bed and stuff," Olivia said with a smile. "We have no problem with another person joining us for as much time as they want to."
"But my friends and family…." Aren said and looked down at the floor.
"I know how you are feeling, Aren," Eliza said and placed her arm on Aren's shoulder."
But life is life.
We can't just predict that everything will go right. At least you have some friends to be with you and support you.
Having friends by your side is a lot better than being and living alone, don't you think?'

"I guess," Aren said to Eliza.

Aren smiled at her.

'Okay, until then, can I be part of you?" Aren asked.

"Yeah, sure!" Eliza answered. "Just watch out for Greg and Sam, who like arguing with each other and SQUABBLING like spoiled toddlers."

"Eliza, are you serious?" Greg asked her, annoyed. "Stop putting our personal stuff in the STREETS like that!"

"WAIT- does that 'personal business' part you said mean that it's TRUE?!" Eliza suddenly asked excitedly.

Sam started talking. "No! It's not like that. What he meant- "

"OH MY GOSH!! OH MY GOSH!!! IT'S ACTUALLY TRUE!!! GREG IS ADMITTING SOMETHING TO BE TRUE FOR THE FIRST TIME IN HIS LIFE!!!" Eliza screamed happily and started crazy bouncing off the walls. Olivia and Aren started laughing.

Then, even though Sam and Greg had been play-teased on the spot like that, they started laughing like crazy, along with Olivia and Aren.

Then after that, Eliza stopped bouncing off the walls, sat on the long couch, and started laughing as well. Everyone was laughing, and there was happy chaos in the fort.

The Call of the Nether   Avya Jain

Soon, the five friends were making jokes and having fun. "Aaaaaand…. The Best Joke Award goes tooooooo…" Olivia announced while cracking up, Greg." She then shouted. "YESSSSSSSS!!!!!!!!" Greg shouted at the top of his lungs.

"I SHALL TAKE OVER THE WORLD!"

He said and then climbed up on top of the end table, with a 'crown' on his head that he had made from a tree's leaves before they teleported to the Nether, saying that it would 'come handy in bossing everyone around and winning 'Best Joke Award'.".

Aren laughed. "I do not really understand how someone who won 'Best Joke Award' would be able to take over the world," Aren said to Olivia while she giggled.
"Well, Greg and 'Best Joke Award' really go together perfectly like best friends," Olivia explained.

"And the second-place winner of the 'Best Joke Tournament' is…. SAM ""CHOCOLATE MILKSHAKE PARTY!!!!!!!!!!!!!!!!" Sam screamed.

He quickly went to his storage cabinet and took five chocolate milkshakes out of his storage cabinet. Then, the group celebrated Sam's 'very smart, recent, and awesome success'.
Soon, the group finished their little chocolate milkshake 'party', and then Sam realized that he had a watch to see the time the whole time.

The Call of the Nether — Avya Jain

"Hey, guys" I just realized I have my watch with me! It shows the time in the Overworld. Imma go get it." Sam said.

With that, he dashed off into his room. Five seconds later, he returned with his watch.
"Hmmmmm……. Now, let me change this to Nether time." But before he could do it, Aren chimed in. "Overworld time is the exact same as Nether time."
"My class did a unit on Nether when I was in third grade," she said.
Sam read the time, "It says Overworld 11 battalions and 7 to avatar morning."

Reader, this basically means 11:07 am. I know that you're like, "Wait, WHAT did Sam just say, the time, or a secret code to unlock a vault that holds the world's rarest diamond?!"

Well, ACTUALLY, it's just the current time in the Overworld and the Nether, as you can see written above somewhere here. But, YES, it IS hard to understand. So, let us proceed farther with this story, after hearing my BORING talks yet AGAIN….

The Call of the Nether — Avya Jain

"Hey guys, if it is that early…" Olivia said. "Why don't we go adventuring?"
"All right?" Olivia said and smiled.
"Perfect Idea!" Eliza announced.
"Of course!" Aren replied.
"**YES!**" Greg said.
"Indeed! Sam yelled.

Okay, reader…… The big moment you were waiting for had finally come. I am sorry I had to make you wait so long. I just wanted to make some attractions so I could get ready for the real thing.
But whatever, put your 3-D glasses on, grab some popcorn and gummy bears, and enjoy the show! **Well, show in a BOOK.**

Chapter 10
The Big Exploration

The next minute, the five friends were packing up for their adventure, which they had been waiting for along with you. They all had their gear on and had their inventories full of everything they needed. Soon, they had set out. Let's go with them! ...

"Where should we go first?" Greg asked.

"Maybe we should go to the site I was on? It's looks pretty fun there," Aren replied.

"Sure! They all responded. And so, they set off. Aren turned into her third form- a swan. She led the way.

But the others didn't notice that when they set off, their portal back to the Overworld reappeared, good as new...

The five of them didn't notice this. Ugh, if only they did, and had some way to keep it there.

BUT WHATEVER! And let's continue...

"It's getting darker as we go," Greg said, shuddering.

"Oh, are you scared?" Olivia asked him.

"What? No! Of Course not. I'm Greg the Great! How can I be scared? He replied and jumped up.

"Cupcake, anyone?" Eliza said as she took out a strawberry cupcake.

"Don't mind if I do!" Olivia said happily and snatched it from her.

"We're here, guys," Aren said as the others looked around the dark site.

"This is where you and your other friends were staying?" Sam asked her.
"It is, Sam," Aren replied. "It actually is. But believe me, it looked like a butterfly garden."
Suddenly, a portal appeared. The group was surprised. Aren turned herself back into her human form. She knew that the huge, dark portal was her own and it didn't know that Aren could transform into a parrot with elegant, long white feathers. So, she decided she would hold onto her secret from the portal, at least. They were even more surprised when the new portal started talking to them.
"I am a teleporting portal, humans," it said. "I know every single one of you. I teleport from place to place, bringing people to the Nether from the Overworld and back. "It said.
"The OVERWORLD?" all the others gasped.
"Yes, the Overworld. I confuse others," it said again.
"Uh, guys? What should we do? Go home or continue adventuring?" Greg asked the others.

The Call of the Nether — Avya Jain

"**ADVENTURING!**" The other four shouted excitedly.

"It's what we came here for in the first place!" Olivia said.

"**OKAY!**" All the others shouted in excitement. They headed in the southern direction. And then, they began their big exploration.

As soon as the group was far from the portal, Olivia decided she would ask a question.

"Um, guys? Do you know if that portal that appeared on Aren's site was ours? Or was it random? Or was it yours, Aren?" Olivia asked.

"Actually, I have no idea," Aren replied.

"I don't know either. All the Nether portals that I've seen before literally look like they've been cloned multiple times or something," Greg shrugged.

"I don't know as well," Sam said. "Maybe it's Aren's, because I'm pretty sure that our portal doesn't talk." Eliza said.

"Wait, I didn't know if my portal could talk too!" Aren said.

"Okay, let's worry about this later, and for now, let's enjoy our adventure!" Greg said.

And so, readers, let's proceed.

Chapter 11
Finding Nether Wart (and other stuff)

The group was excited. More excited than ever. Even Aren, who turned into a swan and directed the group.
The group paused for a break at a corner. Olivia began to talk.
"Guys, we have only seven days, not eight," she said.
"But did not the portal say that we had eight?" Aren asked. She turned back into her normal form.
"We will take one day to clean and destroy our fort. We will take everything that is ours back," said Greg.
"Makes sense," replied Olivia.
Suddenly, the group saw a glowing red-ish light nearby.
"Did we reach the End? It welcomes people with a light like this," Sam said.
"No, I think we reached the end of the Nether," Eliza started.
"What? NO! The Nether is endless! I found that out it in the book I read when we were at the library before we teleported here," Sam said.
Aren went further to check. It's Nether Wart!" she exclaimed.
Neither is helpful in maintaining energy and creating potions. Looks like a medium-sized mushroom that is dark red with a hint of purple.

"Nether Wart is **SO** helpful! And here's an entire garden. An entire stock!" Eliza added.

"Let's take it all," They shouted together.

And so, they split the wart up and set off again.

Soon, they heard voices. The weird part was that they sounded exactly like the group members' voices.

"What? Do you hear that?" Sam asked, confused.

A group came into view; the group looked exactly like theirs!

"**WHAT?**" All five really asked.

"Excuse us, but who exactly are you?" the Real Olivia asked Fake Olivia.

"Um, I think all of YOU guys are impostors," the Fake Aren said firmly.

"I can prove it," the Real Greg shouted.

Quickly, he swung a stick he kept in his backpack stick at Fake Greg. The Fake Greg yelped and fell to the ground and was now in the form of a red pigeon. The fake group suddenly became anxious.

"Who's the fake NOW?" "Asked Greg to the fake group with a mischievous smile on his face.

The fake group screamed loudly in unison and ran until they were out of their sight. The red pigeon flew away as fast as it could.

The Call of the Nether — Avya Jain

"Okay, that was surely weird, don't you agree?" Eliza said.
"Yup," Olivia said.
The group was silent for the next ten minutes.

"Um... guys? Why is it so…... unusually quiet?" Aren asked.
"I don't know; even the Nether isn't this quiet!" Greg replied, his voice is becoming more and more intense.

Suddenly, a waterfall, except the 'water' was lava (you can call it a lavafall) that was in front of them stopped flowing. The group looked around. All the other lavafalls and lava streams were still flowing and flickering. Eliza said "Oh no! I don't remember what the call code was if one lavafall in the Nether stopped working was!" Suddenly, the lava that was in front of them disappeared. But something unusual happened. As soon as the lava disappeared, it caused a minor explosion in which the group couldn't see anything. As soon as the smoke cleared, Sam saw that there were two things lying on the ground: one was a cube-shaped orb that glowed with golden light, and the other was a tiny crystal sculpture that looked like a small box with no lid.
"Is that- Is that supposed to go in there?" Greg asked, as he picked up the orb and the crystal box thing. He then put the orb in the box.

"WAIT-GREG! NO! DON'T DO THAT!" Eliza screamed. She tried to stop him, but it was too late.

Suddenly, the lava reappeared as soon as the crystal and the orb were put together. This time, the lavafall continued to flow, but nearing the end, it split into two and started going in two different directions. The group was devastated by what they saw. It was a secret doorway-a secret doorway hid behind the lavafall the whole time, for who knows how long!

"**WHOA!**" Eliza said in awe. "**Where** does this lead to, I wonder!"

The door wasn't very impressive, since it has been behind a lavafall for who knows how long. It was also burnt and there was smoke pouring out of the gaps in the door. It also had weird stuff dangling around it, and the stuff didn't look like anything they had seen before. Probably some rare stuff. Or maybe even more Nether wart.

"What just happened…?" Eliza was more shocked than ever.

"What is this? Did we reach the End?" Sam asked, part hopeful and part devastated.

"Sam, why are you so desperate to open some sort of weird-looking portal to the End right now when we're in the Nether?" Greg asked Sam.

"Wait, what's a portal again?" Sam asked.

"Sam, WHY? Just, WHY? WHY can't you MEMORIZE something for once?" Eliza sighed.

"What?" Sam shrugged and asked. "You never told me what a portal is. But I do remember what obsidian is."
Eliza rolled her eyes in the direction that Sam couldn't see her doing it.
"But still, why are you so desperate and concerned about the End right now, even if we are in the Nether?" Greg asked again.
"Because I've always wanted to go there?" Sam shrugged.

"WELL, JUST IN CASE YOU HAVEN'T ALREADY NOTICED, WE'RE IN THE *NETHER* RIGHT NOW! WAKE UP! OPEN YOUR EYES!!!" Greg shot back.

"Are you two gonna start SQUABBLING with each other again?" Aren asked.
"Guys, anyways, do you think we should open this door, or leave it closed?" Eliza asked in a whisper.
"Let's open it, I guess," Greg added in a whisper. "I think Sam should do it."
"What? Why ME?!" Sam whisper shouted.
"Just do it, Sam!" Aren whispered. "We've got to see what's behind this door, because we're on an adventure, and we can possibly find some rare stuff!"
"Reasonable enough, I guess," Sam whispered back.
So, Sam took a deep breath, and with the help of the others, pushed the doors and they swung open.

The Call of the Nether — Avya Jain

Suddenly, as soon as Sam and the others pushed the huge iron door open, a voice spoke. "Greetings, adventurers," it said.

The group found the source- a woman with a crown. But they couldn't see her properly because her body and face were all covered in shadows. She was sitting on a throne made of fine diamond, which was the only thing in the big extended lavafall that gleamed. Well, except for the random streams of lava and the torches, which were barely anywhere over here. Anyways, LET'S CONTINUE!

Her voice sounded gentle and fragile.

The Call of the Nether   Avya Jain

"Greetings," the group said back as they entered through the huge doorway. They could see a huge, just-as-gloomy-looking-as-the-huge-door room lit with flickering fire torches and had no random fires just laying everywhere on the floor- but the same bright, orange and yellow lava.

"I know why you have come here," the woman said again." To continue, you must pass my test: An obby."

"WHAT?" Greg shouted in surprise. He turned back the moment Sam grabbed his arm, and the gates slammed shut.

They made such a loud noise that Sam jumped 4 feet high and he started to talk to Greg about how he thought that the Nether was going to break into two pieces. Greg, of course, started to laugh his head off like a maniac at Sam's scaredness. The bright, orange and yellow lava that was now behind the door in their current angle started pouring again.

"Let's proceed with the obby run," the woman said.

And so, they started.

Chapter 12
The (Illusionatic) Obby Run

"You have six days until you have to return back home!" the woman said.
"ONLY SIX?" The group shouted.
The woman got off her throne and waved a hand. Soon, the group could see the Obby. The woman clapped her hands. "Now go, you can do this!" she said.
The obby was all disappearing tiles and pillar jumping.
Now, disappearing tiles and jumping from pillars that are as thick as the wingspan of a butterfly, were sure supposed to be hard, but what the group didn't know was… WAIT, WHY am giving you spoilers? Oh well, let's continue…

"Waaaaait a second…." Greg said. He touched the first pillar, and his hand went right through it.
"It's an illusion!" he cried. The others gasped and looked at the woman with the crown.

"You have passed my first test, but there are still two tests to go," the woman said, toning down. She sounded more serious now. She went and sat on her throne which was made of fine diamond.

She continued. "If you pass these tests, I will gain my image back. Like, my face."
The group felt equally bad for her, so they figured that they would bring her away from the shadows and continue their adventure.

"My second test is for you to find and unlock four chests... The chests can be anywhere." The woman said.
"**WHAT**?! But this place is **HUGE**! It will take SO much time!" Sam groaned.
He looked at the doors. They were still shut, and there was lava flowing on the outside, the same way it had been.
"Well, we have to do it if we ever want to go home," Aren said.
"And also, to bring her away from the shadows."
"You have five days left," the woman spoke.

The group had already run off and split up to look for the chests.

Chapter 13
Chests quests chests quests (tongue twisters are just crazy)

Aren was to find the first chest. She scratched her head, not knowing where the chests were. "I want to find at least one chest so that the others don't start thinking that I'm completely useless," she thought.

It was nearly impossible. The castle/room/dungeon was like an infinite descent. But suddenly, she saw a golden light nearing or behind (should be just nearing) some crates that were near her. So, she went behind the crates to see if there was a chest or at least a key.

Aren pushed a few of the crates over, and on the other side of the stack of wooden crates, there was the first chest! She saw that the chest was delicately embroidered with hearts. She saw the keyhole on the chest, which leaked out some golden steam, and predicted that the key would be around here somewhere, because the chest was right there, in front of her.

The Call of the Nether   Avya Jain

She fiddled with the crates until the key fell out of one of the crates. She unlocked the chest, and a small, grey, stone statue floated out into the air.

Aren did a whoop of laughter and ran off to see the rest of her friends and tell them about the first diamond-encrusted chests being unlocked.

Meanwhile, Sam was struggling too, when he saw a maze that's entry was half-blocked with cobwebs and crates.

He spent twenty minutes in the maze, trying to find chests because he knew that there was a chest in there. He pushed the crates over to the side, and a small ball of white sparkly light appeared.

It started into the maze, and Sam followed it. The ball floated and led to the chest, sure enough. Sam found the key right in front of them and unlocked the chest. It was covered in hearts, just like the chest Aren had unlocked.

He ran out of the maze, with a happy whoop, and unexpectedly bumped into Aren, who told him she had unlocked a chest.

"Great!" Sam said, and so he ran off with Aren to find the others to see if they needed help.

The Call of the Nether — Avya Jain

Olivia and Greg had good sighting skills. So, they found the chest easily. Now, reader, let me tell you this. I'm not trying to say that the others have bad sighting skills.

I'm trying to say that they take a little bit of time to find things like me. But **wait…...** You do not need to know that.

Okay, **WHATEVER**! Back to the **story……**

They found their chest in an old, dismantled cabinet.
But the chest was kind of sealed in with some weird and unique looking cobwebs and other disgusting stuff, so they cut through some cobwebs and got to the key and chests. But boy, that was a thick layer of random disgusting stuff and cobwebs.

They ran to find Eliza, who had just taken a dive into what looked like a pond with purple, enchanted, glowing water. It was near some logs they ran into everyone else. Aren and Sam.
The group found Eliza just as if she was going to jump into the pond-looking oasis of purple, enchanted, glowing water.
They jumped in and saw the chest at first sight. They quickly unlocked it and returned to Ariah. They could see that now her body was visible. But her face was still hidden by shadows.

The Call of the Nether — Avya Jain

"And now, for my final test, you must input four statues that were once humans," Ariah said.

"Who are these once-human statues?" Greg asked, curiously. "I have no idea," Ariah replied. "But even if I did know, I do not have permission to tell you."

So, they started the game. The game was frustrating and difficult because the statues ran away at top speed while the group tried to catch them and input them.

Reader, now I'll tell you a secret.

They didn't notice that when they unlocked the chests, a heart was unleashed from each chest and the hearts flew into the chest of the statues.

Every time it happened, the statue glowed pink for a second and then faded.

The group does not know this, readers. Keep it a secret, for who knows how long! Anyway, after hearing my boring talks, let it continue.

The Call of the Nether   Avya Jain

The group split up and chased after the statues. The statues ran far into the Nether and were nearing the bottomless pits.

The statues were fast. But they lost energy fast, too.

The input test was completed, and the group hurried back to Ariah. But, when they were on their way back to Ariah, a cloud of dust appeared in their path.

"Wait, are we supposed to go through this weird-looking cloud thing of dust?" Sam asked.

"I think we are, if we want to reach Ariah and see if she has anything else planned for us in mind," Olivia shrugged. "Well, also if we want to go home."

So, the group went closer to the dust cloud. Each step they took, it seemed as if the cloud of dust was growing bigger and darker...which made it hard for them to see through the cloud of dust to see if they were going in the right direction of whatever. Then, the group entered the dust cloud, and the dust cloud was dark as midnight now.

"I can't see a thing," Sam squinted. "Is someone next to me right now?"

Greg nudged him.

The Call of the Nether   Avya Jain

Sam jumped. "AAAAAAAHHHHHH!!!!!!!! THERE'S A MONSTER OVER HERE!!!!!! SOMEBODY HEEEELLLPPP!!!!!"

He then came to his senses. "Oh, Greg, it's just you," Sam said.

"What exactly did you think?" Greg couldn't stop giggling.
"Okay, guys, this is NOT the right time for jokes!" Eliza sighed.

"Wait, guys, do I…see the dust…MOVING?!" Aren said.
"WAIT – TORNADO!!!!!!!!!" Sam yelled.

The Call of the Nether   Avya Jain

It was true – a dust tornado was headed right at the group! Now what can the group do?

"RUUNNNN!!!!" Eliza shrieked. But the group was too slow. The tornado came and turned into a massive dust storm. Everything was dusty.

Then, two minutes later, when the storm cleared up, the group saw that they were in front of Ariah. The group saw that she was now in full form. She was so beautiful.

The Call of the Nether — Avya Jain

And they were more amazed than ever. Ariah was now fully visible. She had a beautiful face that(maybe) meant to hypnotize (you know what I mean) people into listening to her every word. Orange maple leaves sprinkled everywhere, which is rare to happen in the Nether, and the gloomy light of the room changed into what looked like something that would only come in fairy tales and dreams. It was like the group was in a dream, except they weren't even close to a dream.

A few minutes later, Ariah's look changed. Her hair settled into a braid, and she disappeared. When she reappeared, her clothing was different, and the look of the fortress changed. It was dark as midnight again, but now it looked like an enchanted garden. Ariah held a ball like stone with glowing golden light coming out of it.

The Call of the Nether

Avya Jain

A lovely smile appeared on Ariah's face. "I thank you, adventurers," she said. "You may now continue with your adventure. But before you go, I want to give you gifts".

Ariah chanted a spell, and pieces of smooth green jasmine rock appeared in their hands.

She escorted them to the Big Gate, which was still closed, and lava was flowing and flickering on the other side. The gates suddenly flew open, and the lava stopped.

The group put the rocks in their inventories and headed off. Ariah spoke before they could go through the door. "Please do not forget me," she said. The group was silent. They looked at each other.

"But if you must forget me," Ariah said. "At least do it with a smile," she smiled.

"Farewell, adventurers".

The group said their goodbyes and went through the door, which now looked like it was something from a dream. The door shut behind them as soon as they were through, and the lava started pouring again.

The Call of the Nether   Avya Jain

It did not look like a secret again, but the group knew it was.

They put a sign next to it with a secret code on it that only the group of five knew, thanks to Olivia, because she read a book called "Make codes that are easy for you to understand but make no sense to anyone else!"

Chapter 14
Back Outside

"My watch shows that we have only three days left, you guys," Sam said.

"Let's do some potion brewing," Greg suggested.

So, they set off to do some portion brewing. They found a brewing stand in a corner.

They brewed potions of every kind -good, bad, strength, enchantments, you name it. They spotted a few blazes, quickly snatched them and used the blaze rods to stir the potions.

They had fun making an enchantments room set to enchantment year, tools and much more.

They laughed till two more days passed, and there was one day left to return home.

"Guys, we have to clean out our fort today", Eliza said to the others.

"**OKAY**!" they all shouted in excitement.

"Guys, I didn't say it earlier," Aren said. "But I think that fort of yours is literally so spectacular. It looks like it would be worthy of being a beach hut, greenhouse, AND a first-place finish if you entered the 'Best Structure Competition' back home!"

"Really? Thanks!" Sam said. "I wish you were there to build with us, because I'm sure you would have some great ideas!"

Chapter 15
Cleaning

(And another two tests DUH!)

The group looked over at Sam. He looked at his watch. "One day and two hours!' He said proudly. "Let's go directly to our fort!" Eliza exclaimed.
She opened her inventory and froze.
"Guys, I cannot find the map! Does someone have a spare map?" Eliza asked.

"I do not!"
"Me neither!"
"I cannot find any!"

"HOW ARE WE GONNA GET HOME NOW?"

Suddenly, the lava flowing outside the secret gateway started to glow even brighter. Then it split going in two different directions. In the open direction a map fell through!

"This might be it," Eliza said.
"Yup, it's it," she said to everyone.
"Wait! Why was our map in a lavafall?" Sam asked.
"I literally have no idea, but let's follow the map," Olivia said.

"Greg isn't talking at all," Eliza said. "Is something wrong, Greg? Or are you just flunked out because I took our book out of your backpack?"

"You WHAT?!?!?!" Greg looked at Eliza.

"Yup, I have your book. I'll give it to you when we're back at the fort," Eliza smirked.
They followed the old-looking map (which was a long journey again) and reached their fort.

The portal was still there waiting, and it was just as happy as they were. It was glowing dark purple. And a few other shades of purple. Maybe even a few pinks. But WHATEVER!...
The group was exhausted. They looked over at Sam's watch.
"It says two days left until the portal disappears," Sam said.
"Two days, right? That means we can get a day of sleep and then we can destroy our fort," Greg said cleverly. Or at least he THOUGHT so, cleverly.

He then stuck his nose in the air. Everyone except Greg did a group eye roll.
So, they entered the fort. Eliza and Olivia worked together to build and fix up a bed for Aren while Sam and Greg cleaned the beds and washed the sheets, blankets and pillows. They also made some space in the storage cabinet for Aren to put her backpack.

The Call of the Nether — Avya Jain

Soon everything was set. The group lay down on their beds. The coolest part about their bed was that their beds were colored- which was rare to do, since there was not much dye anywhere. They slept for a day. They had gotten used to the Nether's day and night - the same looking cycle- and woke up exactly a day later. Thanks to Sam's watch.

"Whew! I feel like I caught up on all the sleep I missed! What about you guys?" Eliza asked. "*yawn* I think so too," Sam yawned.

"Me too".
"Me three, I guess,"
"Me the next. *Yawn*"
"Um, are the rest of you **SURE** that you caught up on all the sleep that you missed?" Eliza asked.

The Call of the Nether — Avya Jain

The other four suddenly jumped. "Yes, we are!" they said.

And so, they destroyed their fort and were done when the portal said that they had four hours left to do whatever they wanted to do.

The group started brainstorming ideas of how to spend four hours.

"Let's have a party to celebrate our recent success!" Aren suggested.

"But… who are we gonna invite? "Sam asked.

An idea popped into Aren's head. "I think we should invite Sam, Greg, Eliza, Olivia and me!" She said.

They baked a cake (I mean **CRAFTED** a cake, or WHATEVER you'll say) and celebrated joyfully with a pizza, since Sam, Olivia, Greg and Eliza had stocked up on two boxes of pizza.

The Call of the Nether

Avya Jain

Chapter 16
What's Wrong with The Portal

The group finished celebrating in two hours. Eliza reminded the group that now they had two hours left.
"We can play around for two more hours now!" Eliza said, excitedly.

"But… I wanna go home" Greg said.
"Me too!"
"Me three!"
"Count me in!"

Eliza was outvoted one to four. So, they decided to pack their bags.
As soon as they did, the portal welcomed them to jump through. But as soon as they jumped across the portal, , they saw that everything was still the same blazing fires, Netherrack floor.
The group was horrified. "We're still in the Nether!" Greg cried.
"Um, I think we can all see that," Sam said, annoyed.

WAIT- WE'RE ACTUALLY STILL IN THE NETHER!

"Yeah, so what did you think? That I was lying to your '**UGLY FACE**' you saw was **YOUR** face!" Sam shot back.
Okay, reader, I'll put it this way…

The Call of the Nether   Avya Jain

Greg: "No, point in arguing with you. *Rolls eyes in one direction*"
Sam: "Okay, **NO POINT IN ARGUING WITH YOU, EITHER!** *Rolls eyes in other direction*"
Aren: "............"

Eliza: **"WILL THE TWO OF YOU STOP SQUABBLING LIKE SPOILED TODDLERS?"**

Olivia: Can the two of you apologize to each other? Because this portal is staring at us all like we have the IQ of a mud puddle! With slugs in it!"
Portal: "Ermmmmmmmmmmmmmmmm…….."
Greg: "Alright, **FINE**, I'm sorry, Sam, but – "
Sam: **"APOLOGIES DO NOT HAVE 'BUTS'!"**
Greg: "HAHAHAHAHAHAHAHAHAAHAHHAHAHA!"

The Call of the Nether — Avya Jain

Everyone else: "HAHAHAHAHAHAHHAHAHAAHA!"
Sam: "Ughhhhhhh!"
Okay reader, that mode is **OVER**.
Okay, so where were we? Oh right, the portal was not working.
"Wait… we jumped through you!" So why are we still in the Nether? Aren asked the portal.

"You failed my test," the portal said, trying not to giggle.

"WHAT? WHAT TEST?! YOU DID NOT TELL US ABOUT SOME RANDOM UPCOMING TEST!" Greg exploded.

"I tried to give you a warning when the two of you were fighting," the portal said, "but then I thought, 'Let me test their cleverness.'"
"What do you mean, test their cleverness? YOU DIDN'T EVEN GIVE US CLUES!!!!!" Greg shouted.
"Okay, whatever, so now how are we going to get home?" Eliza sighed and asked the portal.
Not that easy, Portal replied.

All of them looked at each other with a disappointing face, holding their heads off and screamed- "What NEXTTTT"??

Chapter- 17
Keys Hunt

"To get home, you must find three purple keys and throw them through me all together." the portal replied.
"Ummm…. okay," the others said.

The keys can be anywhere in the Nether," the portal explained.
"WHAT?!?!?!?!?!?!?!?!?!?!?!?" Greg shouted. "WHAT DO YOU MEAN?! WE ONLY HAVE HALF AN HOUR TO GET THOSE KEYS!!! HOW ARE WE GONNA DO THIS?!?!?!?"

"The keys aren't in the endless pits," the portal said. "And that's the only clue I can give you.
You want to go home, don't you?"
"Okay, but how long is this gonna take?" Eliza asked the portal
"It'll take as much time as it will. I can't predict the time, because the Nether is HUGE," The portal said.
"Then we shall not waste any of this valuable TIME!" Sam said.

With that, the group dashed off together.

The Call of the Nether — Avya Jain

A while later, they came across a bridge that was half broken.
"Wait…do I….see...a KEY?!" Eliza said.
"How do we get it? It's on the other side of this broken bridge. I don't want to risk jumping!" Sam said.
"Wait…maybe that's IT! We should JUMP and get to the other side!" Eliza exclaimed excitedly.

"WHY did I say that?" Sam sighed. "I don't wanna jump!"
"Come on, don't be a scaredy cat!" Eliza teased him.
So, they had no choice but to jump. Sam was the least enthusiastic about jumping across the bridge.

Sam jumped. He screamed. "AAAAAAAHHHHHH!!!!!!"

And then, he landed safe on the other side! "Sam, why were you so scared? Nothing happened!" Eliza said to him.
"What? How would I know if the bridge had a huge bulging gap or whatever?" Sam rolled his eyes.
"Anyways, guys, here's the key," Aren said. She picked up the key. The key was purple, with white sparkles swirling around it. Suddenly, the sparkles started to swirl faster and brighter with every swirl. It was as if the key was saying, 'Use me. Use me now!'

"Wow, guys, this key actually looks really cool!" Aren exclaimed.

"I actually agree," Greg said. "So, Sam, how shaken up are you?"

"Who said that I was shaken up?" Sam asked.

"You did," Greg shrugged. "In fact, you said it just now."

Sam slapped his forehead.

"Anyways, guys, we found the first key," Olivia said. "Let me put it in my backpack for safekeeping."

She took the key from Aren and put it in her backpack.

"We still have two keys to find," Greg said. "Let's get to it!"

The group continued walking straight.

Soon, they spotted a few…glowing crates. Very unusual.

And, near those crates were…. some cobwebs. Very unusual again. Well, COBWEBS near stuff like LEGENDARY GLOWING RARE CRATES is unusual.

But again, near the glowing crates, there was some… white light. And a hint of purple.

"WAIT- that means there could be another key somewhere near those glowing crates!" Eliza exclaimed.

She went forward and pushed the crates over. They fell and made a BANG.

Smoke poured out of the crates. Everything disappeared.
Soon, when the smoke cleared, everything reappeared. Eliza said, "Um, guys… What. Just. HAPPENED!!!!!!!"
"I have no idea!" Sam exclaimed. "Wait, THAT'S THE KEY!!!!!"

Sam pointed to a key that looked the same as the one they found when they jumped from the broken bridge.
It was the same shade of purple, with the same swirl of white sparkles that became faster and brighter. Eliza picked it up and put it in her backpack for safekeeping.
So, they set off again.
"Guys, when is that portal gonna disappear?" Sam asked. "Do any of you know?"

"Nope," Eliza said. "Speaking of portal, we have to find the last key so that we can go home!"
A while later, the group saw a funny-looking cliff. On the other side, they saw a golden light.
"Come on! Maybe the key is there, so should we go check?" Sam asked.
"Dude, are you serious right now? We'll have to look everywhere we can to find this last key so we can get out of here!" Greg replied.

The Call of the Nether — Avya Jain

The group started to climb up the cliff. It was hard, since there were boulders rolling down the cliff at top speed. One boulder almost knocked Aren off the cliff, but she dodged it just in time. Then, another huge boulder came rushing at Sam.
Now, Sam was scared of boulders that came right at him. Greg knocked it away before it could hit Sam's head. Sam was really touched by Greg's gesture and hugged him in the moment.

A while later, they all reached the top of the towering cliff and noticed that there was a chest on top of it. Golden light leaked out of the holes.
The chest was old and worn with cobwebs. Sam took out his sword and cut away all the cobwebs.
Then, they opened the chest.
As soon as they opened the chest, it turned into a new-looking chest, as if it had just been crafted. The key was inside, and it was the same as all the other keys.
  "GUYS!" Greg shouted. "WE FOUND THE LAST KEY!!!!! NOW WE CAN FINALLY GO HOME!!!!"

Then, the chest disappeared as soon as Eliza put the last key in her backpack. Then, a sugary-looking crystal that looked like a small box with no lid and a cube-shaped orb appeared where the chest had been.
"Wait- these things are like the ones we found when we found the secret door!" Sam exclaimed. "Are we supposed to put them together, like last time?" Aren asked.
"I think we are," Olivia said.

The Call of the Nether   Avya Jain

Olivia picked up the crystal and the orb. She put the orb in the box-shaped crystal, and it exploded, but there wasn't any smoke. There was some sort of blue glow.

After the glow cleared, another chest appeared. "I'm gonna open this chest!" Greg exclaimed.

He opened it and the group was whisked right back to where their fort had been.

"Great job, adventurers," the portal said.

Eliza opened her backpack and took out the keys. Then, she threw them through the portal and the portal started glowing a dark purple. It invited them to jump through it. The group was so happy to finally be going home after what seemed like a few million years. But Aren was the happiest and most excited of them all.

After collecting everything that they owned and saying farewell to the Nether, the group jumped through the portal. After the entire group was in, the portal disappeared in the fastest, brightest, and happiest swirl of purple.

Chapter 18
Back to Paradise

In the blink of an eye, the group was back home to their community. technology, blah blah blah.
Everyone was super happy to finally be home. But Aren was the happiest.
All of them were happier than ever. The group of four high-fived each other and stepped through the portal again.
"Okay, guys! Let's split up. Do you know where you are going, Aren?" Eliza said.

The portal teleported them and they were coincidentally outside Aren's house. Aren's parents came running outside and saw Aren standing right there.

"Yup!" Aren was beaming.

"This was just amazing!" Greg said.

The Call of the Nether

Avya Jain

Next, they arrived at their houses. "Is this where you are supposed to be?" the portal asked.
"Yup," Eliza said to the portal. "
"Wait! Before you go, I would like to give you a gift," the portal said.
Shining, sweet-smelling rose quartz appeared in each group members' hands.
"Goodbye," the portal said.
It glowed again. Then in a swirl of purple, the portal disappeared.

"OH MY GOSH!!! Did this portal actually give us ROSE QUARTZ?!?!?!?!?!?" Olivia screamed happily.

"Um, I think so," Sam said.

"Rose quartz is literally SO RARE!!! It's SO hard to find!! If you want to find it in the underground mines, you will have to dig REALLY deep!!" Olivia replied, annoyed with Sam.
Sam just rolled his eyes.

"Anyways, guys, we should go back home so we should plan something, don't you think?" Eliza suggested.

Okay, sure," Sam replied.

So, readers, they split up and went in different directions, well, until they reached their homes. They were really happy to finally be back home. But they were the happiest about the fact that they had the opportunity to do something awesome, thrilling, and mysterious, like going to the Nether.

This adventure was just....

MORE EPIC THAN EPIC!!!!!!!!!!!!!!!!!!!!!!!!!!!!!

Chapter 19
Dinner Party

The group went straight to their bedrooms and had a virtual meeting with each other.
They planned a dinner party with lots of fun and food for their parents and them. They decided to have it in the afternoon. So, the plan was official and finalized to be held at Olivia's house.
The afternoon came by quickly. The four agreed that they wanted to hold on to this quickly passing time.
The dinner party started with Eliza telling some stories. The sun was setting beautifully and being in the sunroom made the sunset look even prettier.

Eliza had started the story some time ago.

"......and then, we saw Ariah's face and boy she was beautiful!" Eliza exclaimed to the parents during the dinner party.

Just as she was about to reach the end of her sentence, the group heard a scratching noise coming from outside the window.

The group and parents looked up at the high window and saw a swan. For some reason, to the group, the swan looked vaguely familiar.

It was Aren! Aren had come over. She waved her wings to say hello. The group said their hello back to her by giving her a wave. Then she smiled down her thanks and flew away.

"Who was that?" Eliza's mom asked. "It seems like you know her".

"She is our newfound friend from Nether," Eliza explained. "She's just an ordinary girl, but she can transform into a swan. And, a white parrot

"WHITE parrot?" Sam's mom asked.

"Yeah, a white parrot is a unique parrot that can only be found in very limited places," Eliza explained again. "White parrots are rare. Or actually, I think that's the first white parrot that ever existed."

"But I'm gonna resume with my story now!" Eliza said.
An hour later, Eliza was almost done with her story.
"And so, that nice, talking portal gave us rose quartz chunks that were the size of a stone you would find on the beach, and then it disappeared in a swirl of purple!" She spoke.
The group then held out the pieces of rose quartz that they had received from the portal. They also took out the smooth green jasmine rock that they had received from Ariah. The parents were so surprised.
"I love these rocks because now I can add them to my rare rocks collection!" Greg exclaimed.

"Well, I love them because now I can use them to decorate my room!" Eliza said.

"I like these rocks because I can put them on my dresser!" Sam exclaimed.

"I love them because they are my very own!" Olivia said.
"A talking portal that gives rocks as gifts?" "Sounds crazy, doesn't it?"
Olivia's mom asked.

The Call of the Nether — Avya Jain

Soon, they were all eating dinner of a choice of spaghetti or pizza. Sam chose the seat next to Greg (although Greg didn't welcome it) mainly to annoy him.

"What was your favorite part of the adventure and back, you guys?" One of the adults asked.

"My favorite part was seeing our newfound friend go home!" Greg said.

"My favorite part was playing that SUPER fun, SUPER cool, and SUPER mysterious 'Find the chests' game," Olivia said.

"My favorite part was winning the argument with Greg!" Sam said proudly.

Greg quickly shot Sam the death stare. Sam literally jumped.

"My favorite part was, well, about the Nether," Eliza said.

"What about the Nether?" Eliza's mom asked.

"We wouldn't have been there if one small thing did not invite us," Eliza replied.

"What small thing?" her mom asked her again.

"The call of the Nether," Eliza beamed.

"If the Nether never called to us, we would have never been there".

The Call of the Nether — Avya Jain

The entire group beamed their best. Their parents clapped louder than ever.

Shall we too clap for the group that survived the most dangerous place in the history of the Overworld?

Well, one of those people are us, so let's clap for ourselves too, and be proud of the gifts we received along the way from Ariah and the portal, the smooth green jasmine rock from Ariah and the light pink sweet-smelling rose quartz from the portal.

Along with this group, we love adventuring and having fun with our five new friends and seeing Sam and Greg fight their for-no-reason-at-all fights, which makes you and me laugh a lot, and brings all the entertainment that we can ever possibly get. Let's be proud. Prouder than we have ever been.

But **WAIT**.......

If you thought our adventure here was **OVER**, you ain't read **NOTHING** yet!

The group left the Nether, all right. But a secret didn't leave the Nether yet.

The Nether began to glow red, then, a woman appeared, with a crystal ball.

"So, they've been here, huh?" she said to herself.

"Well, they've clearly disturbed my home. I'll haunt them so that they don't ever come back. And they got rid of my problem parrot too."

With that, she set off.

Wait a second… PROBLEM PARROT?!?!?!?!?!?!?!?!?!?!?!?!?!??!?!?!?!?!?

What is happening? Is this Problem Parrot Aren? Or is it someone or something else? Oh well……

TO BE CONTINUED………

Printed in Great Britain
by Amazon